PYRAMIDS

© Aladdin Books Ltd 1989

Designed and produced by
Aladdin Books Ltd
70 Old Compton Street
London W1V 5PA

Library of Congress Catalog
Card Number: 88-83093

First published in the
United States in 1989 by
Gloucester Press
387 Park Avenue
New York, NY 10016

ISBN 0 531 17154-X

Back cover: An Old Kingdom sculpture
showing a dwarf and his
family.

Design: David West
Children's Book Design

Editor: Catherine Bradley

Illustrator: Gerald Wood

Map: Aziz Khan

*The author, Anne Millard, had a Ph.D in Egyptology from University
College, London. She is the author of numerous books on Ancient Egypt.*

*The consultant, George Hart, is the Education Officer at the British
Museum in London.*

Printed in Belgium.   All rights reserved.

Contents

HISTORY HIGHLIGHTS

PYRAMIDS

GLOUCESTER PRESS
New York · London · Toronto · Sydney

INTRODUCTION

On the edge of the Western Desert, west of Cairo, Egypt, is the Giza Plateau. There stand three colossal stone pyramids which were one of the seven wonders of the ancient world. These pyramids were built over 4,500 years ago during Egypt's Old Kingdom. They have survived remarkably well although they have all lost the fine outer layer of stones.

The first thing that strikes you when you look up at the Giza pyramids is that they are truly gigantic! The tallest one is 485 feet (148 m) high. When the Arabs invaded Egypt, they called the pyramids "the mountains of the pharaoh." There are more than 70 other pyramids in Egypt and Sudan. Who built them? Why did they go to so much trouble? What were they for? How did they organize and pay for such a staggering task and what was it like to live then? In this book we try to find some of the answers.

Near the Great Pyramid of Giza the remains of a ship were found dismantled in a pit. It was to take the pharaoh to the next world. Experts have now rebuilt it.

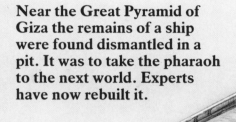

TYPES OF PYRAMIDS

STEP
The first pyramids to be built were like this. Only one still stands. It was designed by the court official, Imhotep.

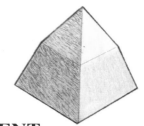

BENT
This was probably a mistake! Its sides were too steep so it had to be finished at a different angle.

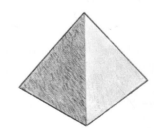

STRAIGHT-SIDED
The first straight-sided pyramid to be planned and built was for King Sneferu of Dynasty IV.

WHY PYRAMIDS?

Pyramids were built to be the permanent tombs of Egypt's kings. Some queens also had pyramids but theirs were very much smaller. Old Kingdom pyramids were built along a stretch of desert, some 29 miles (48 km) long, just west of the city of Memphis. Memphis was Egypt's capital at that time. Now the city has been ruined and buried.

The Egyptians believed pyramids would protect the body of the King and the goods he was taking with him into the next world from robbers. But pyramids had another job to do as well. They were the place from where the soul of the king would go to the sky. Spells written on the walls of later pyramids reveal this. Step pyramids were built as staircases to heaven which the king would climb to reach the stars. In Dynasty IV there was a change in religious beliefs and straight-sided pyramids were built as sunbeams made of stone up which the king would walk to join the sun god.

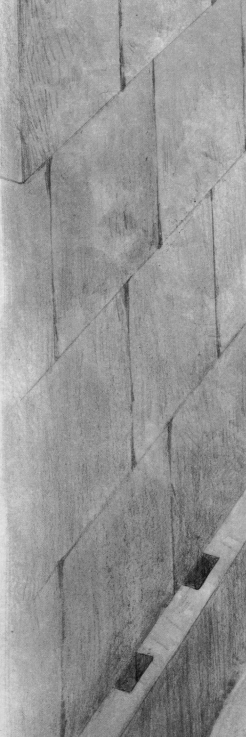

Here the king's body is being taken to its last resting place. The Egyptians did not use wheeled carts so the coffin was dragged on a sled. The coffin was made of stone and cedar wood. The priests chanted prayers because they believed these would help the king up to heaven.

THE GODS

The Egyptians worshipped many gods and goddesses. In the Old Kingdom the most important were Re-Harakhte, the sun god, Horus, the sky god, and Hathor, the Great Mother. Ptah was the great craftsman, who created the universe. The common people became very fond of Osiris, their god of the dead, and his loving wife, Isis. Many of the gods had animal heads and human bodies.

Re-Harakhte Horus Hathor Ptah Osiris Isis

6

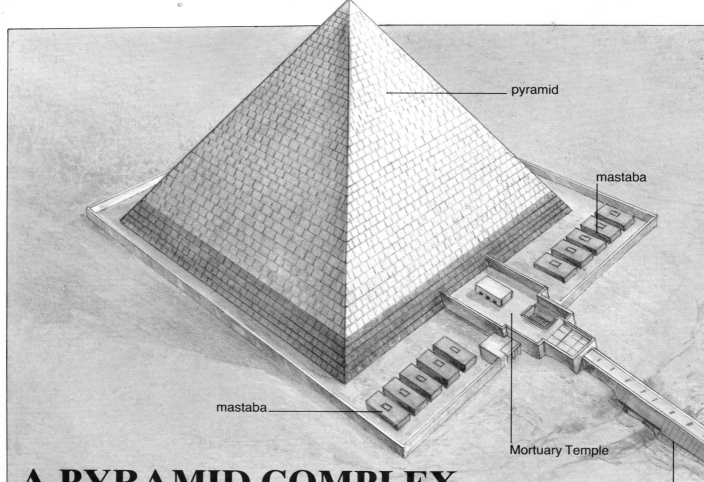

pyramid

mastaba

mastaba

Mortuary Temple

covered causeway

A PYRAMID COMPLEX

Where the desert met the cultivated land of the valley, the Valley Temple was built. There the king's body was prepared for burial and rituals were conducted so his soul could enter his statues and enjoy the offerings placed before them. A causeway (a very long corridor) led up to the Mortuary Temple, built against the east side of the pyramid. There, every day, offerings of food and drink were made for the king's soul. Large estates provided the king with all the provisions he would need for eternity.

The entrance to a pyramid was usually on the north side. From there a passage led down then up to the burial chamber, which was at the center of the base. Apart from one or two side chambers, the rest of the pyramid was solid. A pyramid did not stand alone. Around it were the tombs of the king's family and courtiers. These were smaller rectangular tombs we call mastabas. The queen might have had a small pyramid of her own.

The biggest pyramid of all is at Giza. It belonged to King Khufu of Dynasty IV and it is known as the Great Pyramid. There were several changes of design during its building so it ended up with three chambers, as you can see in the cutaway picture on the right. Only one chamber was used for burial.

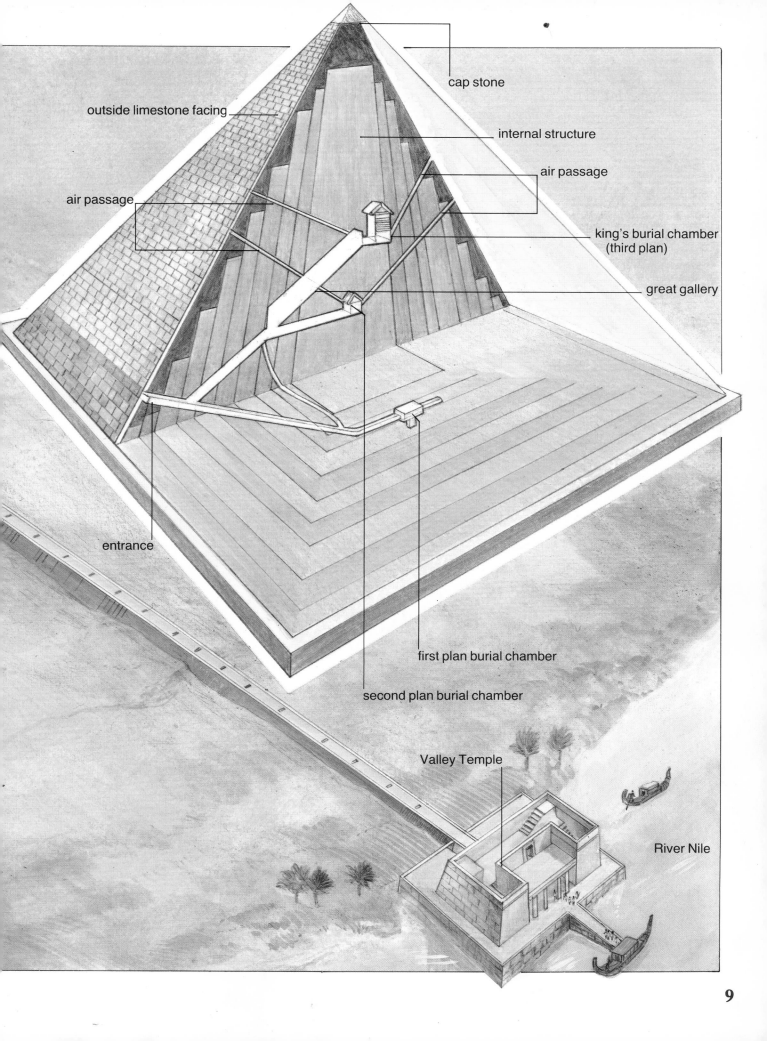

cap stone

outside limestone facing

internal structure

air passage

air passage

air passage

king's burial chamber (third plan)

great gallery

entrance

first plan burial chamber

second plan burial chamber

Valley Temple

River Nile

9

FURNITURE

This chair belonged to Queen Hetepheres, the wife of King Sneferu and mother of King Khufu. It was made of wood covered with gold. Although the wood had decayed, archaeologists were able to reconstruct it from the gold that remained. Pictures in nobles' tombs also show what furniture in the Old Kingdom was like.

THE GOD KINGS OF EGYPT

Egyptians loved parties with lots to eat and drink, dancers, music, acrobats, storytellers and magicians. Here the king and queen relax with some of their family.

We sometimes call an Egyptian king pharaoh but to his subjects he was the King of Upper and Lower Egypt. He was more than just a powerful man, who united the once independent kingdoms of Upper (South) and Lower (North) Egypt. He was thought to be descended from the sun god Re. It was also believed that the spirit of the god Horus could enter him. This meant he was a unique being, a link between gods and men.

The king had absolute power over his people. In his palace he was protected from the gaze of ordinary people. He was surrounded by servants and officials, many of whom were members of his own family. They carried out his orders. Because of their divine ancestry, only the king's own sisters were good enough to be queens.

11

BUILDING PYRAMIDS

The pyramids were not built by slaves or prisoners of war but by ordinary Egyptians. Because money had not yet been invented, people paid taxes to the king by giving him goods and, at certain times, working for him. When the harvest was safely stored away, thousands of peasant farmers paid their labor tax by helping to build their king's pyramid.

They used sleds and ropes of papyrus (a water plant) to drag the stones into position. Once the bottom layer was in place they built a ramp and brought up the next layer of stone. The ramp was made longer and higher as the pyramid rose. When the top had been reached the whole pyramid was covered with a casing of fine white limestone and the ramp was removed. The masons who cut the casing stones of the Great Pyramid were so skillful that you cannot get a sheet of paper between the stones.

The people worked quite happily because the king fed and clothed them while they labored for him and they knew the work would please the gods. They also believed that, just as the king looked after them in this world, so he would care for them in the next. It was thus very much in the laborers' interests to ensure he got safely into the next world!

THE GIZA PYRAMIDS

Dynasty IV (c2613-2494 BC) kings built the largest pyramids, of which the most famous are the Giza Plateau ones. The kings who built at Giza were:

Khufu (also known by the Greek version of his name, Cheops). His was the first of the Giza pyramids. It is called the Great Pyramid as it is the largest of all. It was finished in about 2565 B.C. It was known as a wonder of the ancient world because of its great size and near perfect pyramid shape. King Khufu had it built to protect his belongings for eternity. However robbers were able to break into it and steal its contents. Later on, in the Middle Ages, people took its outer casing stones away to make buildings in Cairo. Khufu also built some smaller pyramids for his wives. Only the pyramids survive of his pyramid complex – the mastabas, causeway, and temples have all disappeared.

Khafre (the Greek version of his name is Chephren), was the builder of the second pyramid. He was Khufu's son. This pyramid was finished in about 2545 B.C. Although it only slightly smaller than the Great Pyramid, because it was built on higher ground it looks as if it is the same size.

Menkaure (the Greek version of his name is Mykerinus) was the builder of the third pyramid. It had to be finished in a hurry with mud bricks. Its Valley Temple contained a very fine collection of statues.

There are three small queen's pyramids beside Khufu's and three more beside Menkaure's.

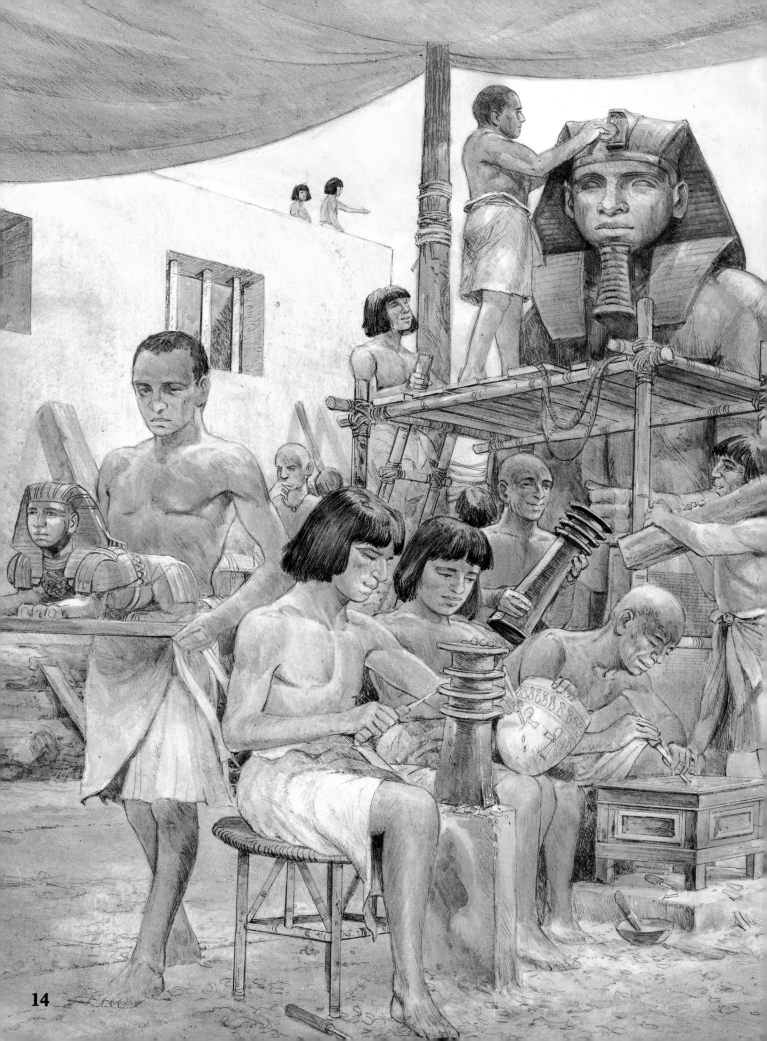

CRAFTSMEN

Pictures on the walls of nobles' tombs often show craftsmen making the goods that their masters would need to keep them in comfort throughout eternity. Overseers kept an eye on the work to see it was all up to standard while scribes kept records so no one stole anything!

A small but important group of people in Egypt were the craftsmen. They worked in groups producing the magnificent statues and elegant furniture, the graceful stone vessels and delicate jewelry which were used in the palaces, temples and villas of Egypt. Others built boats, worked in leather, made ropes and bricks.

Stone, semi-precious stones, gold and copper could be found in Egypt. The Giza pyramids were finished with casing stones of limestone from across the Nile. Good timber and silver had to be brought in from foreign lands.

Women were usually in charge of spinning and weaving the flax that made the linen cloth for Egyptian clothes. The best cloth was so fine that it was almost transparent.

The best craftsmen were employed by the king, the temples and the nobles. They were paid for their work in food, beer and wine, linen and oil which they could use or exchange for other goods.

JEWELRY AND TOOLS

This is a falcon made out of gold with obsidian used for eyes. It was probably part of a statue and was found at Hierakonpolis. It shows the art of the goldsmiths.

Iron and bronze were not in use in the Old Kingdom, so craftsmen used tools made of stone, copper and wood. Here are a few of the tools found in tombs.

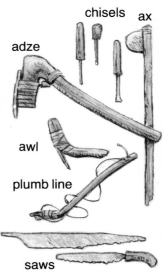

chisels ax
adze
awl
plumb line
saws

DAILY LIFE IN EGYPT

The reason the kings could afford to build the pyramids was that Egypt was a wealthy country thanks to its farming. Every summer the River Nile burst its banks and flooded the land. Not only did it bring much needed water but also a new layer of rich soil that was left on the fields after the flooding was over.

The Egyptians learned how to store the flood waters and carry them to their crops through a network of canals and ditches. Crops were planted in October after the flood went down and grew during the winter. The harvest was in March and April. The wheat was reaped by hand. Then men drove oxen over it to separate the grain from the straw. Women did the winnowing, that is, they tossed the grain up so the husks would blow away. The grain was then stored.

An Egyptian harvest in progress. Most Egyptians were peasant farmers. They worked on the lands belonging to the king, the temples, the nobles or to the great funeral estates. They had to pay part of the crop to the landowner. The farmers kept sheep, goats, pigs, cattle, donkeys, ducks and geese.

A FARMER'S HOUSE

Because temples and tombs were meant to last forever, they were built of stone. Houses for the living, whether a palace or a farmer's hut, were built of mud bricks that had been baked in the hot sun until they were hard. The little house on the left is based on models placed in tombs at the end of the Old Kingdom. The house is small. The people spent a lot of time on the roof enjoying cool breezes or they worked in the courtyard. Grain was kept in silos.

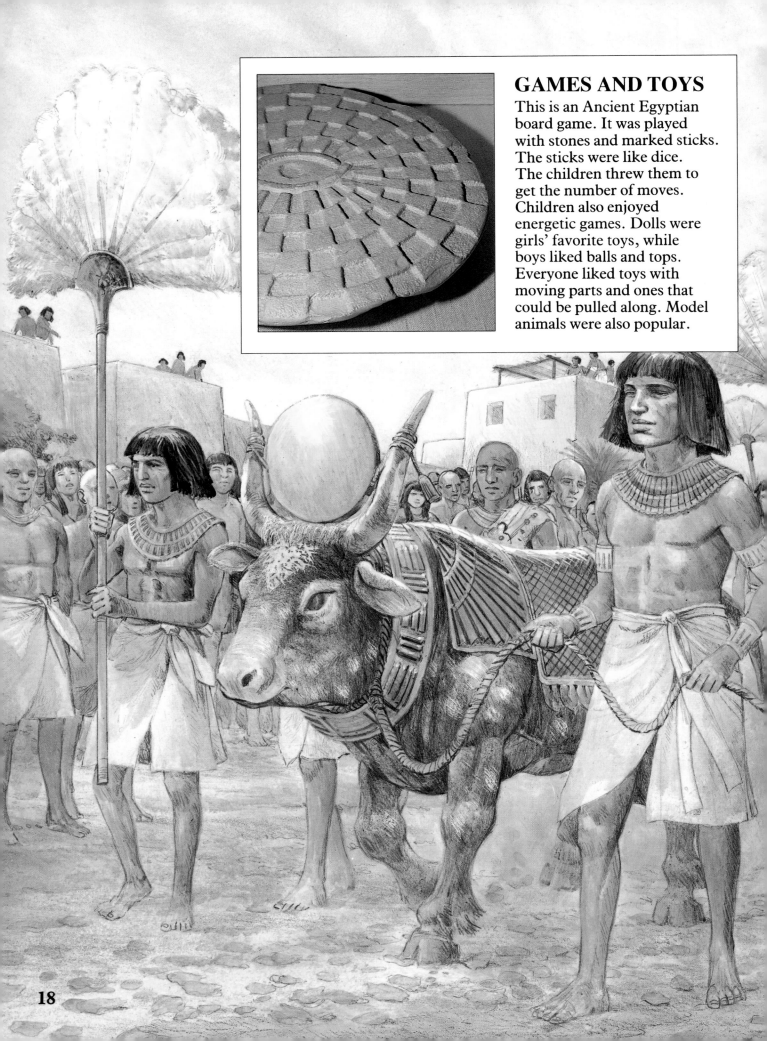

GAMES AND TOYS

This is an Ancient Egyptian board game. It was played with stones and marked sticks. The sticks were like dice. The children threw them to get the number of moves. Children also enjoyed energetic games. Dolls were girls' favorite toys, while boys liked balls and tops. Everyone liked toys with moving parts and ones that could be pulled along. Model animals were also popular.

GROWING UP

Egyptians had to work hard but they knew how to enjoy themselves. Many religious festivals were held. This is the festival known as the "Running of Apis" when the god Ptah sent his spirit into a specially chosen black and white bull. As the bull was led out of the temple the people rejoiced.

Ancient Egyptian parents gave their children plenty of time to play. But even in the rich land of Egypt, farmers had to work hard to survive. This meant that by the age of seven, children were doing simple jobs to help their family.

Unless specially chosen by their lord, children of the Old Kingdom had little chance of going to school. The girls were taught by their mothers how to cook, spin, weave and do other tasks. Cooking consisted of preparing bread, beer, meat, fish and many vegetables. Meanwhile boys were taught by their fathers how to be farmers or craftsmen. Parents chose the husbands and wives of their children. Marriages took place when they were very young – about 15 for a girl and a bit older for a boy. By the standards of the day Egypt had good doctors, but even so life was often short and people wanted to live it to the fullest.

SCRIBES AND SCHOLARS

About the year 3300 B.C. the very first examples of writing appeared in Egypt. The use of writing was a vitally important step in the development of any civilization. It meant people could accurately pass on information and thoughts to future generations without relying on people's imperfect memories. The Egyptian system of running the country involved keeping very detailed written records of everything. The ones who did the writing, the scribes, were very important. In the Old Kingdom, however, a family had to be well off to be able to send a child to school.

Egyptian scholars were famous for their wisdom. They were especially good at medicine, mathematics, engineering and studying the stars. The most famous scholar was Imhotep who designed the first Step Pyramid for King Zoser and was worshipped as a god by later generations.

Scribes and artists cover a tomb wall with texts and pictures. First a grid has been painted on the wall to act as a guide so that every line obeyed the strict Egyptian rules about size and shape. Pictures and hieroglyphs were carved out and painted.

HIEROGLYPHS

Egyptian writing signs were small pictures which we call hieroglyphs. There were several hundred signs. Some have the value of one letter, while others stand for two or more letters. The scribe could write from left to right, from right to left, or in vertical columns.

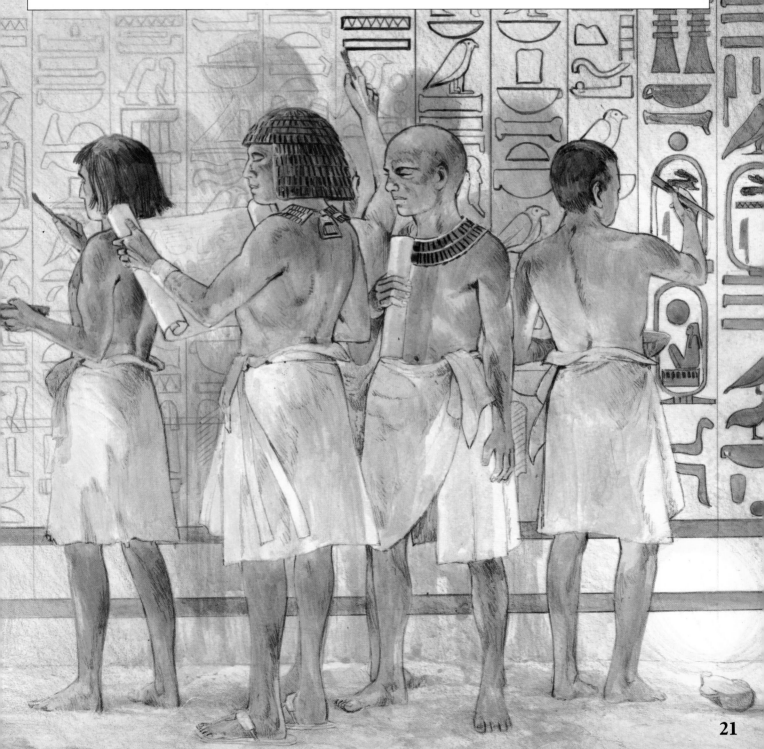

21

MUMMIES

△ The picture above shows the wrapped body of a noble found in the tomb of Nefer. It is one of the few Old Kingdom remains to have survived.

▽ The picture below shows the mummy of King Seti I. By the time he was buried, the Egyptians had perfected their skills in preserving bodies. After his tomb had been robbed, the priests secretly reburied his body. The body was not rediscovered until 1871 A.D.

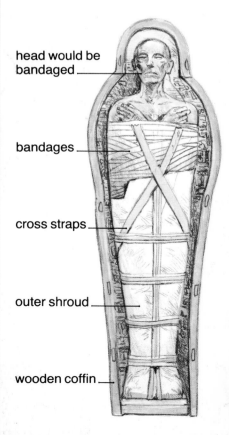

head would be bandaged

bandages

cross straps

outer shroud

wooden coffin

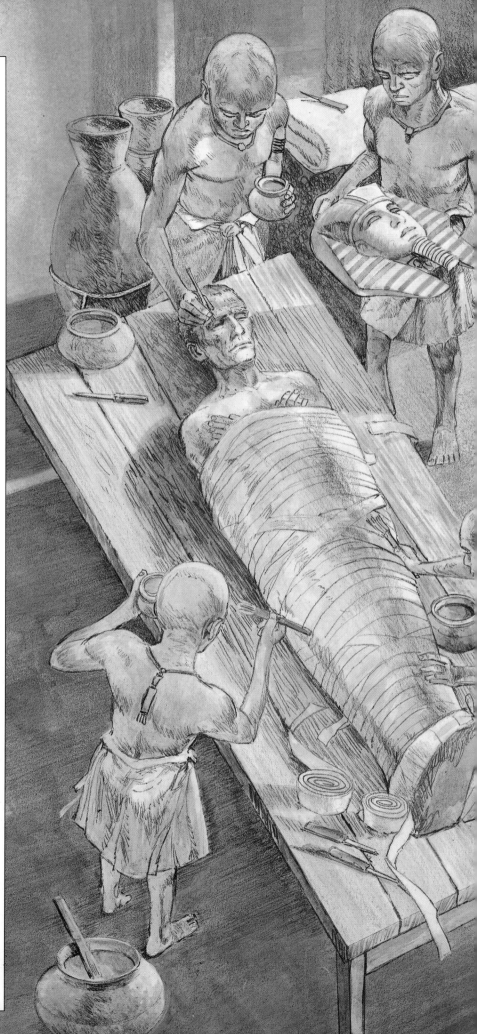

THE NEXT WORLD

Egyptians believed that death was just a gateway to an eternal life in the next world. The kings would join their relatives, the gods, and every day would sail across the sky with the sun god in his sacred boat. The ordinary people would dwell in a land in the West. If they had lived a good life on earth, they would enjoy a happy time in a place that was like Egypt but was without any problems.

Egyptian people believed that after death they would need food and drink and all the other necessities of life. These could be provided either by offerings or by pictures in tombs, which came to life when the right prayers were said. But in order to enjoy all this to the full, they believed that it was necessary for their bodies to survive too and this posed a problem because human bodies naturally decay.

To preserve the body after death, the Egyptians used the process of mummification. Only the bones of the Old Kingdom mummies have survived. First the embalmers removed some of the body's internal organs. Then they washed the body in preserving salts and wrapped it.

23

THE NILE – EGYPT'S LIFELINE

Nobles would go out in their papyrus skiffs with harpoons to catch fish and even hippos and crocodiles for sport. They also used to throw sticks to catch the wild birds that lived in the reeds by the river banks. Those who caught fish and birds for a living used nets – they needed large quantities to sell in the market.

Without the Nile there would be no Egypt but a desert, because it almost never rains there. Only the land which was flooded could be cultivated. Pyramids and graveyards were built on the desert edge so they did not take up any farming land. But the Nile gave Egypt more than just water. It provided fish, reeds and water fowl and was the main route of transportation.

THE NILE TODAY

The Nile is as vital to Egypt today as ever. Now the great Aswan Dam controls the flood waters and makes electricity. The temples at Abu Simbel were threatened by the dam so they were rebuilt on higher ground. The river is still used for carrying heavy loads – machine parts as well as stone – and tourists sail up and down to visit the ancient sites.

Egypt is a long, narrow country with the Nile flowing down the middle. To shift the massive quantities of stone needed to build a pyramid, the Egyptians waited until the flooding so they could float the stones right up to the desert edge and save unnecessary work hauling them across the fields.

Papyrus reeds were useful for making small river boats. Larger ships were built of wood. The best timber was cedar from Lebanon (on the Mediterranean coast). The Egyptians had to import wood regularly.

WHAT HAPPENED TO PYRAMIDS?

Towards the end of the Old Kingdom, pyramids got smaller and were less well made. They had small rough blocks of stone and rubble inside instead of the fine big blocks used at Giza. The Old Kingdom ended in civil war and chaos and, despite all the dangers and difficulties, robbers broke into the pyramids. They stole the treasures and destroyed the kings' bodies.

In the Middle Kingdom order was restored, and in Dynasty XII a new line of powerful kings built themselves pyramids. They were made of mud bricks with a casing of stone. The builders used many tricks to hide the burial chambers from robbers, but none worked and later kings gave up building pyramids.

Some New Kingdom nobles and even middle class craftsmen began to build tiny pyramids over their tombs, but it was not a style that lasted long. Then, far to the South, in what is now the Sudan, the local kings, heavily influenced by Egypt, began building brick pyramids as their tombs.

Thieves break into the tomb of a long-dead king. When the kings' rule was weak, men began robbing tombs. It was a crime punishable by death. But the treasure in the royal tombs and even in nobles' tombs was so rich that the robbers could not resist.

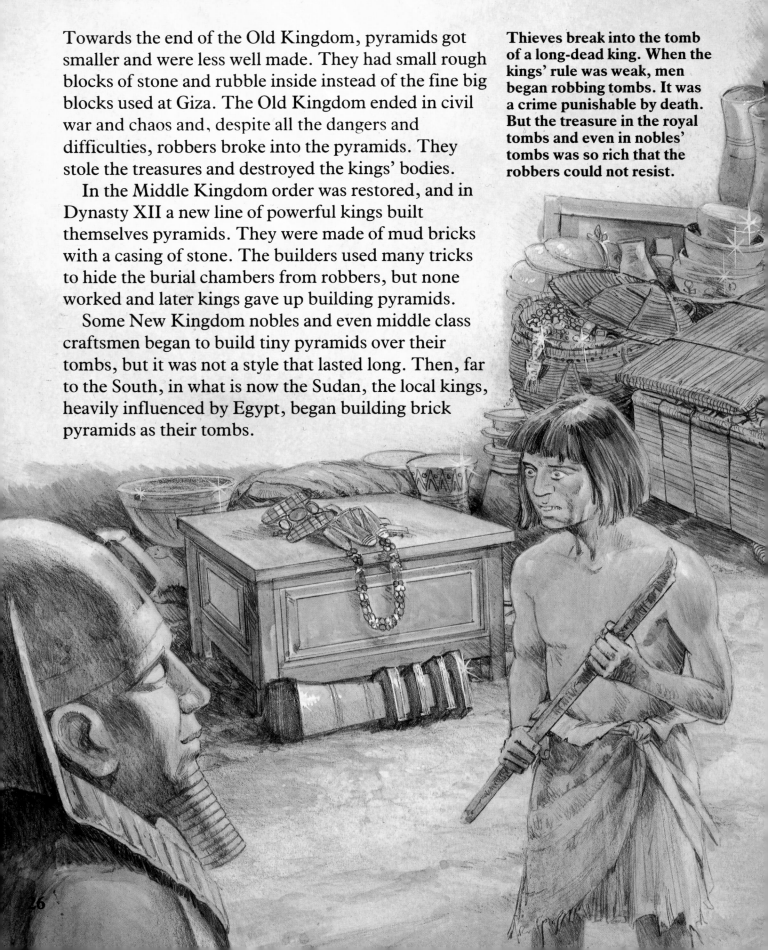

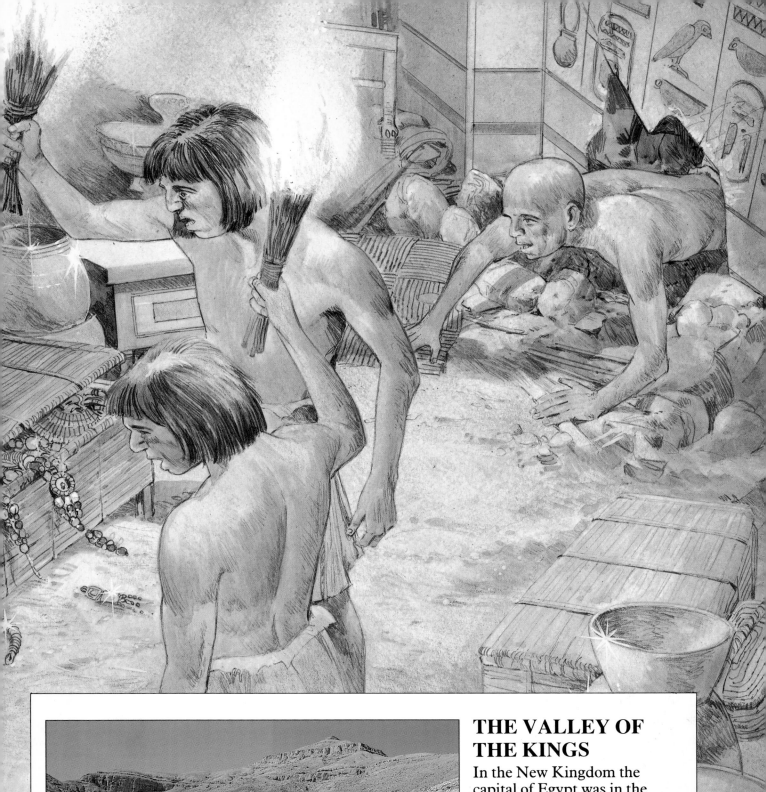

THE VALLEY OF THE KINGS

In the New Kingdom the capital of Egypt was in the southern city of Thebes (modern Luxor). The kings were buried there in rock-cut tombs in the Valley of the Kings. They may have chosen this place because the mountain that towers above is pyramid shaped. The Kings probably wanted to be buried beneath this sacred symbol.

27

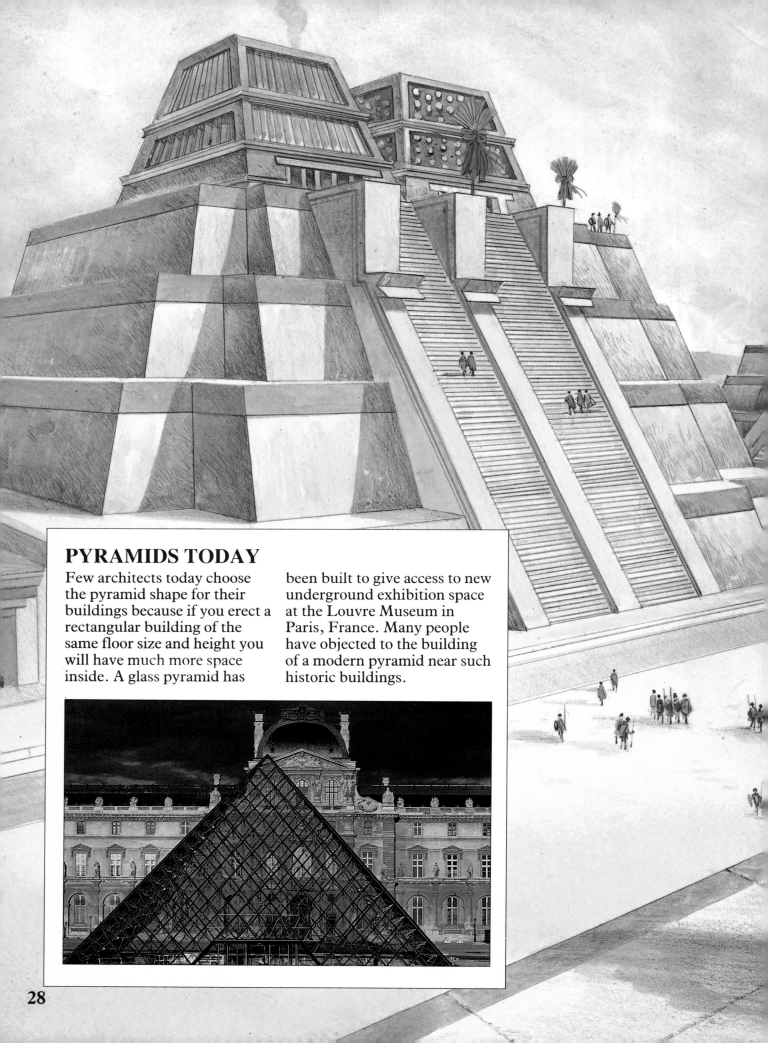

PYRAMIDS TODAY

Few architects today choose the pyramid shape for their buildings because if you erect a rectangular building of the same floor size and height you will have much more space inside. A glass pyramid has been built to give access to new underground exhibition space at the Louvre Museum in Paris, France. Many people have objected to the building of a modern pyramid near such historic buildings.

PYRAMIDS WORLDWIDE

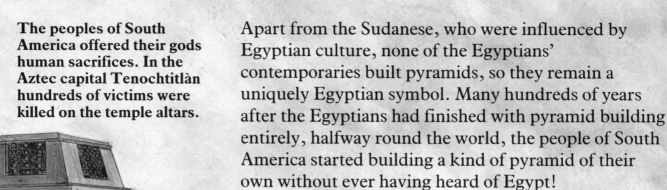

The peoples of South America offered their gods human sacrifices. In the Aztec capital Tenochtitlàn hundreds of victims were killed on the temple altars.

Apart from the Sudanese, who were influenced by Egyptian culture, none of the Egyptians' contemporaries built pyramids, so they remain a uniquely Egyptian symbol. Many hundreds of years after the Egyptians had finished with pyramid building entirely, halfway round the world, the people of South America started building a kind of pyramid of their own without ever having heard of Egypt!

The great stone pyramids of the Incas of Peru and the Aztecs of Mexico had flattened tops, not points as in true pyramids. They had steps that led to the flat tops where they built temples to their gods. South American pyramids therefore look completely different from Egyptian ones and were built for a different purpose. The Incas and Aztecs were at the height of their power toward the end of the period which we call the Middle Ages in Europe.

DATE CHARTS

MEDITERRANEAN SEA

All dates for the Old Kingdom are approximate.

c. 5000-3100 B.C. Predynastic Period. Small communities of farmers gradually united to form two kingdoms – Upper and Lower Egypt. The King of Upper Egypt wore the White Crown and his capital was Hierakonpolis. The king of Lower Egypt wore the Red Crown and his capital was at Buto.

c. 3100-2686 Archaic Period (Dynasties I-II). Menes, King of Upper Egypt, conquered Lower Egypt and united the two lands. He built a new capital at Memphis. Royal tombs of mud brick mastabas built at Abydos and Sakkara.

c. 2558-2533 Khafre rules Egypt.

c. 2533-2505 Menkaure is Pharaoh.

c. 2181-2040 First Intermediate Period (Dynasties VII-X) Collapse of kings' rule; wars and famine.

c. 2040-1684 The Middle Kingdom (Dynasties XI-XIII) Egypt reunited by a Prince of Thebes (modern Luxor).

c. 1684-1567 Second Intermediate Period (Dynasties XIV-XVII). Another period of chaos. Invasion by foreigners we call Hyksos, who ruled northern Egypt.

▲ **Pyramids**

Sais

Alexandria

Buto

Tanis

LOWER EGYPT

The Delta

(CAIRO)

Red Crown

GIZA ▲

Memphis

SAKKARA ▲

Fayum

River Nile

RED SEA

White Crown

● Abydos

● Thebes (Luxor)

Valley of the Kings

UPPER EGYPT

● Hierakonpolis

● Aswan

● Ist Cataract

EUROPE

▲ Paris (Louvre)

ASIA

AMERICAS

▲

AFRICA

▲ Aztecs

▲ Incas

c. 2686-2181 The Old Kingdom (Dynasties III-VI). One of the greatest period's of Egypt's long history.

c. 2686-2613 King Zoser

c. 2613-2589 Sneferu ruled Egypt.

c. 2589-2566 Khufu becomes Pharaoh.

c. 1567-1085 The New Kingdom (Dynasties XVIII-XX). Hyksos driven out by the Princes of Thebes, who then ruled a united Egypt from Thebes. Kings buried in rock-cut tombs in the Valley of the Kings at Thebes.

c. 1318-1304 Seti I is Pharaoh.

NUBIA

N

SUDAN

AFRICA	ASIA	AMERICAS	EUROPE
3000 B.C. Egypt already a united nation. Metal and writing both in use.	**3000 B.C.** City states in Mesopotamia, using metal and writing. Farming in China.	**3000 B.C.** Corn cultivated by South American farmers.	**3000 B.C.** People of France and British Isles building stone circles. Development of metal industry in Greece and Crete.
2700 Beginning of Egyptian Old Kingdom. Step pyramids built.	**2700** Silk weaving and bronze work in China. Indus Valley culture in India develops.		
2600 Straight-sided pyramids built.		**2600** Temple mounds on coasts of Peru.	
2500 Increasing drying up of Sahara.	**2500** Growth of cities in Indus Valley. Use of writing. Cotton cloth made there. Royal Graves of Ur.	**2500** Improved farming and weaving techniques. Use of irrigation.	**2500** Bell beaker culture.
	2300 Sargon of Akkad unites southern Mesopotamian cities into an empire.	**2300** Pottery in Mesoamerica. In Mexico farming people build permanent villages.	**2300** Bronze Age.
	2230 Akkad invaded by Gutians.		
2150 End of Old Kingdom			
2000 Beginning of Dynasty XII		**2000** Early Eskimo culture stretches from Greenland to Siberia.	**2000** Main building phase of Stonehenge.
			1900 Construction of great palaces on Crete. Use of writing.
	1800 On the Steppes, horses first used to pull carts, then used in Near East to pull chariots. Rise of Babylon. Hsia dynasty rules in China.		
1700 Middle Kingdom collapses. Hyksos invade.			
	1600 Hittites settled in Anatolia. They form an empire from the Mediterranean to the Persian Gulf.		**1600** Rise of Mycenae (Greece).
1550 New Kingdom established.		**1550** First metal working in Peru.	* Note: all dates are approximate.

INDEX

Photographic Credits:
pages 10 and 23: Robert Harding Library;
page 12: Michael Holford; pages 14, 17 and 26: Peter Clayton; pages 20 and 21: British Museum; page 27: Rex Features; back cover: J. Allan Cash Library.

PRINTED IN BELGIUM BY
proost
INTERNATIONAL BOOK PRODUCTION